To myself

"Look on my works, ye
Mighty, and despair!"

Percy Shelley's Ozymandias

Blood

Metallic. Basic. Impure. Intimate.
Addictive. Bonding.
All from me.
Monthly attack of me.
All I ask is to be pooled by it.
Consumed by my own shedding.
Sentient to necrotic.
Narcotic non existence.
Pain, pain, pain.
Heat and clot and nothingness.
Flowing to rigid.
Let the washing water be the
only dynamic.
Let the white cloth be the only pure.
Finite attack.
Let the soil be filled with ritualistic
primitive tears and I resistant.

This reminds me of an old
womb's existence.
Of a burial.
When my body rots into the salt
of the earth.
Something sweet.
I'll try to smell my uterus to
simulate death.
I'll try to numb the mind for now.

Why do I act?

Why do I act like I'm motherless?
Like I am fatherless and landless.
Like my soul is immortal.
Like my neuroses can survive
another day.
Like I am indispensable.
Like I have no creator to turn to.
Like I have no grave to be buried in.
Like my friends are a given.
Like my self-love is a religion.

I am mortal

I am mortal yet endless
Recreating my mother's
beginning and mine
I arch I gasp
She arched she screamed
I sin she blesses

Erotic

The erotic is dark
Shadow of a hidden hand
Sacral and sacred
Sweet and sinful

Dos and do nots

I do not sing of drunken nights
or lust-filled odysseys
I sing of paradise as if god
spoke it to me.
Of things not mentioned in
the Quran.
I write sins, tragedy,
and humanity.
I don't write inauthenticity
I bleed from my heart
But that means that I am alone

Ivy

Ivy birthed poison.
From its vein it pumped red.
Ivy birthed poison.
Carcasses reek.
Ivy birthed poison.
Her mistake.
Poison she bled never
turned into elixirs.

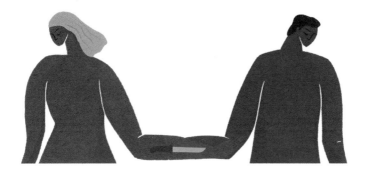

Father

Father sharpen the blade 12th month.
How time is bleeding
Have your premonitions clued
you on your disobeying fruit
He doesn't want your sacrifice
Neither sweet nor fresh
Tainted defiled
Does your faith help you keep
a steady hand
She'll hide her wailing like
she always does
Waxing moon chased
If release is guaranteed
Is it true?
Can we be free?
All knowing father order mine
No mercy needed for a damned one.

Sapphires

Sapphires glow in the dark.
I hear mitski on my vinyl.
Glowing pink.
It's activated so sweetly at my base
inside of me pulsating.
With every beat of the pink my chest
aches with deafening scratches.
They meet each other halfway yet
willing to go the distance.
My palms and arches lose to gravity.

Pride

The poison of pride my
parents fed me.
Arrogance to arrogance.
Never to be wronged.
Beware the wrath of a
woman othered.
If they hit, I hit back.
Til it's dust to dust

Anger

I vow muted anger.
Never to be heard
Melting my atria
Fusing my ventricles
The fire deep within me can never
be exterminated
I vow diamond anger
Carbonated mess
Pressure sores

Wrist

Obsessive awareness of my wrist.
Do I miss tight time or crave an incision
When you fantasize the infliction,
is it with a knife or a razor?
Hair pulling isn't something major, I say
But my wrists ache for my sake
A warning.
Psychosomatic infiltration.

A Spiral

My thoughts are killing me.
Inwards a spiral
Guilt from guilt.
I dreamt of a fire so vast
it consumed me.
I slept another day.

Vinyl

Pain in vinyl
Immortalized
A relic of tears: Solidified
Loneliness: Ostracized
Do you hear jet black from
the record player?
is it familiar to your soul?
I yell cliches and I want
to be heard
Yet echo fills my hallways
like an old friend

To my nose

To my big nose
My aquiline nose
My fat nose
My deviated septum
My mother's nose
My grandmother's nose
my hooked nose
my mocked nose
my nose

Rhythm

How many times can I abuse rhythm?
Silence infiltrates
My sanity's vulture
Where is my anesthetic?
Broken vinyl
Abandoned guitar
Background filler
Cathartic muses

My body

Pinkish on my olive hue
Dangling silk black
Enticing kind browns
White and brown and hairy
Green lines on my wrist
You're the being of my soul
You're what society has
wanted me to hate
But I celebrate

My bed

She lays within me.
Wraps her body around mine.
Weighty and tremor-like.
Should only come to me
to enjoy me.
Her selfish sorrows, burns me
with hot tears and deafens me
with cracks of what should be
a broken back.
Taller than me.
She brings anger.
Her desperate need for comfort.
What do I have to offer?

End of times

I fear the end of times.
But I fear the pain of
tomorrow even more
When will the angels breathe?
I crave the magic of catharsis
The mythicality of death

Devil

Sometimes I feel so bad,
I compare myself to the devil.
The devil I rebuke on the daily.
Tarot says I am it.
January 15th.
I feel the prayer call calling
for my spirit.
I dream dreams crying to saints
about the devil's hold on me.

Woman

My mother told me a story of a
woman from my people's land
Caged, unwanted
Flesh, exoticized
Shame, personified
I demand an exorcism
A relief from all that is killer.

Gifts

I don't accept gifts in fear
of love being tainted.
My parents traded in gold for glitter.
Can I ever love if not by diamonds?
Materialistic memories.
Can I ever love?
Will Venus ever pour her
diamond rain on me?